The Holy Spirit POWERED LIFE

BRUCE DOWNES

The Holy Spirit **Powered** Life Daily Devotional Series
© 2025 by Bruce Downes

For more information contact

Bruce Downes Ministries
PO Box 55750
Phoenix, AZ 85078
(602) 612-9705
BruceDownes.org

CONTENTS

INTRODUCTION TO THE
HOLY SPIRIT POWERED LIFE SERIES

Have you ever wondered if there is more to faith than what you're currently experiencing?

More than going through the motions. More than simply believing. More than attending church and hoping to feel something. Deep in the heart of every believer is a desire to know God, not just with the mind, but in a real and personal way. That longing is the whisper of the Holy Spirit.

The Holy Spirit is not a concept. He is not distant. He is not reserved for a few. The Holy Spirit is the living presence of God - given to every believer - to transform, empower, guide, and renew. And when we open our hearts to Him, everything begins to change.

This 6-week devotional series is a journey into that transformation. *The Holy Spirit Powered Life* is divided into three key themes:

Weeks 1–2: Experiencing the Power of the Holy Spirit

Weeks 3–4: How to Grow the Fruits of the Holy Spirit

Weeks 5–6: The Trinity and the Holy Spirit

Each day contains a scripture passage, a reflection grounded in Church teaching, a prayer, and a journal prompt to help you respond. These reflections are not about theological complexity. They are about spiritual depth. They are an invitation to grow, not just in knowledge, but in intimacy with God. The Daily Devotionals are to help you with your prayer life.

You don't have to be perfect to begin. You just need to be open. The Holy Spirit meets us in our weakness, speaks into our silence, and walks with us step by step.

Whether you are brand new to this or have journeyed with the Holy Spirit for years, this is your invitation to go deeper. To be refreshed. To be filled. To live a life shaped, empowered, and led by the Spirit of God.

So, take a breath. Begin in prayer.

Come, Holy Spirit.

Let this be the beginning of something new.

EXPERIENCING
the POWER of the
Holy Spirit

INTRODUCTION

Pentecost changed everything. In a single moment, the disciples moved from fear to courage, from waiting to witnessing. The power of the Holy Spirit transformed ordinary people into world-changers, not through force, but through divine presence.

I'm inviting you to begin again. Whether you've walked with God for years or are returning after time away, this is your upper room moment. Over the next six weeks, you'll be invited to encounter the same Spirit who came in fire and wind who still comes today.

You won't be asked to strive, but to open your heart. To pray, **"Come, Holy Spirit."** To discover the strength that meets you in weakness, the voice that speaks in silence, and the peace that surpasses understanding.

This is not about a one-time experience. It's about beginning a journey of living in the power of the Spirit every day.

DAY 1 – THE SPIRIT COMES

Devotional Reflection:

Pentecost is not just the Church's birthday. It is a bold declaration of what happens when the Holy Spirit fills ordinary people. That day in the upper room changed everything. Once-fearful disciples were transformed into courageous proclaimers. A scattered group became the Church. A hesitant voice became the Gospel on fire.

Scripture tells us, "When the day of Pentecost had come, they were all together in one place" (Acts 2:1). And then the unthinkable happened. "Suddenly from heaven there came a sound like the rush of a violent wind… Divided tongues, as of fire, appeared among them… All of them were filled with the Holy Spirit."

That one moment fulfilled Jesus' promise in John 14. "I will ask the Father, and he will give you another Advocate… he will be in you." The same Spirit that hovered over the waters at creation, that descended on Jesus at His baptism, now came to dwell within His followers. Not just alongside, but within.

The Catechism teaches that Pentecost "marks the beginning of the age of the Church" (CCC 1076). It was not a one-time event. It is an invitation. The Spirit who came then still comes now. The Spirit who empowered them empowers us.

Many of us long for more. More joy. More direction. More power to live faithfully. Pentecost tells us it is not something we manufacture. It is Someone we receive.

So today, do not rush past it. Pentecost is your invitation to begin again. Wherever you are, however, ready or unready you feel, pray the ancient prayer the Church has always prayed. Come, Holy Spirit.

Journal Prompt:

Where do you most need the Holy Spirit to "come" in your life right now? Write a prayer of invitation from that place.

"When the day of Pentecost had come, they were all together in one place... All of them were filled with the Holy Spirit and began to speak in other languages, as the Spirit gave them ability."
Acts 2:1, 4

Prayer:

Come, Holy Spirit.

Come into the room of my heart, like You came into that upper room.

Blow through the fear, the doubt, the weariness, the waiting.

Fall on me like fire, burning away what holds me back, lighting a flame that cannot be hidden.

Make me bold. Make me willing. Make me Yours.

Just as You changed them, change me.

Father, I ask this in Jesus' name, through the power of your Holy Spirit.

Amen.

DAY 2 – FILLED AND TRANSFORMED

Devotional Reflection:

The coming of the Holy Spirit at Pentecost was not just a moment of supernatural spectacle. It was a moment of deep interior transformation. Peter, who only weeks earlier had denied Jesus out of fear, now stood up and boldly proclaimed Him as Lord. What changed? The Spirit had filled him. And that same Holy Spirit is offered to us today.

Transformation is one of the clearest signs of the Spirit's presence. Not just outward change, but the kind that reshapes our thinking, softens our hearts, and gives us strength to live the Gospel when we would rather shrink back. The Spirit comes not only to comfort, but to convert. Not only to inspire, but to empower.

The Catechism says, "The mission of Christ and the Holy Spirit is brought to completion in the Church... the Spirit prepares men and goes out to them with his grace, in order to draw them to Christ" (CCC 737). It is the Spirit who enables us to live the life Jesus calls us to. Without Him, we grow tired. With Him, we are renewed.

Pentecost was never meant to stay in the upper room. It spilled out into the streets. The Spirit did not just stir the disciples. He sent them. If we are filled but not changed, we may have missed what the Spirit came to do.

Maybe you feel like Peter before Pentecost, timid, uncertain, a little shaky in your faith. That is exactly who the Spirit came for. You do not need to be perfect. You just need to be open. God does not ask you to pretend. He simply asks, "Will you let me fill you?"

Journal Prompt:

In what area of your life do you most need transformation right now? Ask the Holy Spirit to begin His work there today.

"All of them were filled with the Holy Spirit and began to speak in other languages, as the Spirit gave them ability... Peter, standing with the eleven, raised his voice and addressed them."
Acts 2:4, 14

Prayer:

Holy Spirit, fill me today.

Come into the places of fear,

where I feel small and uncertain.

Make me bold like Peter, not because I am strong, but because You are with me.

Change my heart. Renew my mind.

Strengthen my spirit.

Let Pentecost not just be a memory in the Church's past, but a reality in my present.

Fill me so fully that Your presence overflows into the lives of those around me.

Father, I ask this in Jesus' name, through the power of your Holy Spirit.

Amen.

DAY 3 – THE SPIRIT FOR EVERY DAY

Devotional Reflection:

It is easy to imagine Pentecost as a once-in-history spiritual high point. Fire, wind, tongues, boldness, something dramatic and distant. But the truth is, Pentecost was not meant to be an exception. It was the beginning of how every believer is called to live. The power of the Holy Spirit was not only for the apostles. It is for every disciple. That includes you.

Too often we treat the Holy Spirit like a guest who visits occasionally, not a companion who walks with us daily. Yet Jesus said clearly, "I will not leave you orphaned... I will ask the Father, and he will give you another Advocate, to be with you forever" (John 14:16,18). Not for a moment, but forever.

The disciples didn't just receive the Holy Spirit at Pentecost and go back to life as usual. Everything changed. They prayed differently. They saw people differently. They endured suffering differently. Why? Because the Holy Spirit was no longer just among them, but within them.

Jesus promised the Holy Spirit as a constant helper. Not just a visitor for spiritual highs, but as the One who dwells within us. That means the same power that raised Christ from the dead is available to you on a Thursday afternoon just as much as it is on a Sunday morning. The Spirit gives us power to live, faithfully, quietly, consistently, when we feel we have little strength of our own.

You don't need to wait for the "right" spiritual moment. You are a temple of the Holy Spirit, and that makes every moment holy. He comes to fill the surrendered heart, right in the middle of your real, messy, beautiful life.

Journal Prompt:

Where in my daily routine can I pause to acknowledge the Holy Spirit's presence?

"But you will receive power when the Holy Spirit has come upon you; and you will be my witnesses..."
Acts 1:8

Prayer:

Holy Spirit, help me to walk with You my everyday life.

Teach me to recognize Your voice in the ordinary moments.

Open my eyes to see where You are already at work around me and within me.

Give me a heart that listens, hands that serve, and a spirit that trusts You deeply.

Let Your presence in me bring peace and purpose to everything I do today.

Father, I ask this in Jesus' name,

through the power of your Holy Spirit.

Amen.

DAY 4 – THE SPIRIT SPEAKS

Devotional Reflection:

One of the most beautiful mysteries of life in the Spirit is that God still speaks. He is not silent. He is not distant. He is not only recorded in Scripture but present through the Spirit, guiding us moment by moment.

The Holy Spirit is not a vague feeling or abstract force. He is a Person, the third Person of the Trinity, who teaches, reminds, corrects, and leads. Jesus said, "When the Spirit of truth comes, he will guide you into all the truth… he will declare to you the things that are to come" (John 16:13). The voice of the Spirit may not always be audible, but it is unmistakable. Often it comes as a quiet conviction, a deep sense of peace, or a prompting that aligns with the character of Christ.

In the Book of Acts, the Spirit directed the Church with clarity. "Set apart for me Barnabas and Saul," the Spirit said in Acts 13, sending them into mission. The early Church knew how to listen.

Sometimes people ask, "How can I know if it's really the Holy Spirit?" A few things help. The Spirit never contradicts Scripture. He never speaks in fear, shame, or confusion. His voice leads toward love, courage, and truth. That's why stillness matters. The Spirit does not shout over noise. He waits for our attention.

God still speaks. The question is not whether He is speaking, but whether we are listening. As St. John Henry Newman wrote, "God has created me to do Him some definite service… I am a link in a chain." Listening to the Spirit is how we find our next step in that chain.

Journal Prompt:

When have you sensed God speaking to your heart? What helped you know it was Him? Write a prayer asking the Holy Spirit to teach you to listen more attentively.

"When the Spirit of truth comes, he will guide you into all the truth… He will glorify me, because he will take what is mine and declare it to you."
John 16:13–14

Prayer:

Holy Spirit, help me to hear Your voice.

Speak truth into the noise and stillness of my life.

Lead me in the way I should go and give me a heart that listens with faith.

Quiet the distractions, the doubts, and the fear that make me second-guess Your leading.

I give You permission to guide my next steps and remind me of everything Jesus has said.

Teach me to listen with expectation and obedience.

Father, I ask this in Jesus' name, through the power of your Holy Spirit.

Amen.

DAY 5 – STRENGTH FOR THE STRUGGLE

Devotional Reflection:

The presence of the Holy Spirit does not mean the absence of struggle. In fact, some of the deepest work the Spirit does in our lives happens not when everything is easy, but when life is difficult.

In Acts 4, after Peter and John were arrested and threatened for preaching about Jesus, they returned to the other disciples and prayed. But they did not pray for safety. They prayed for boldness. And the Spirit answered. "When they had prayed, the place in which they were gathered together was shaken; and they were all filled with the Holy Spirit and spoke the word of God with boldness."

Sometimes we think if the Spirit is with us, things should be smooth. But the Holy Spirit does not always remove the hardship. He gives strength within it. He gives courage where there was fear. Endurance where there was weakness. Hope where there was despair.

The Catechism reminds us that "it is in the trials that the Spirit brings about growth in holiness" (CCC 2015). This is the mystery of God's grace, that the fire we face can refine us, not destroy us, when the Spirit is with us.

You may be walking through something right now that feels overwhelming. But you are not alone. Ask the Spirit to give you boldness. Not to escape, but to endure. Not to be spared, but to be strengthened. The Spirit did not abandon the early Church in difficulty, and He will not abandon you.

Journal Prompt:

Where in your life do you need boldness or strength right now? Write a prayer asking the Spirit to fill you with courage and peace in that place.

"When they had prayed, the place in which they were gathered together was shaken; and they were all filled with the Holy Spirit and spoke the word of God with boldness."
Acts 4:31

---

fri 8/29

Prayer:

Holy Spirit, give me courage.

In the middle of my struggles, come and strengthen me from within.

Where I feel anxious, bring peace.

Where I feel weak, bring endurance.

Let my faith grow even when life is hard.

Help me to keep going when I want to give up.

You are my Comforter, my Advocate, my Strength.

I trust You to carry me through.

Father, I ask this in Jesus' name, through the power of your Holy Spirit.

Amen.

DAY 6 - A TIME OF PRAYER: COME, HOLY SPIRIT

Devotional Reflection:

As we come to the end of this first week, we pause, not to review, but to rest. To breathe. To enter into the quiet space where God meets us not in our striving, but in our stillness.

All week we've reflected on the power and presence of the Holy Spirit. We've seen how the Spirit came at Pentecost, how He fills ordinary people with extraordinary strength, how He transforms weakness into witness.

But now, on this day of prayer, we are invited not just to reflect, but to respond. Not with more words, but with surrender.

Come, Holy Spirit.

This is our simple prayer. Our honest desire. That the Spirit who hovered over creation, who fell upon the disciples, who lives within us, would come afresh again.

This is not a moment to achieve something. It is a moment to receive.

Maybe you've felt His presence this week. Maybe you haven't. But He is near. He is with you now. The Spirit

Sadezo

doesn't need perfect conditions. He only needs a willing heart.

So today, slow down. Light a candle. Take a walk. Sit quietly. Listen to worship music. Whisper His name. Create space. And as you do, trust that the Spirit will fill it.

Prayer Focus:

Spend time today in silence. Begin by repeating the ancient prayer: **Come, Holy Spirit.**

Invite Him into every part of your life, your thoughts, your fears, your hopes. Ask Him to come not only to you, but to your family, your church, your community.

"All of them were filled with the Holy Spirit."
Acts 2:4

Closing Prayer:

Come, Holy Spirit.

Come into my waiting. Come into my rest.

Come into the places I have opened this week
and the ones I still hold back.

Breathe new life into me. Stir a deeper hunger.

Fill me again with Your presence and peace.

Today, I make room for You.

Father, I ask this in Jesus' name, through the
power of your Holy Spirit.

Amen.

DAY 7: GO DEEPER ON SUNDAYS

As you journey through this devotional, I invite you to take a
step further each week by watching the weekly Sunday message
on our website. These messages are prayerfully prepared to
encourage and deepen your walk with God. Join me as we
reflect more fully on the theme and allow God to speak into
our lives in a powerful way. Watch on our website
[BruceDownes.org] 8-3)

DAY 8 – OVERFLOWING WITH THE SPIRIT

Devotional Reflection:

When the Holy Spirit comes into our lives, it is never meant to stay bottled up. The Spirit overflows. He fills us so completely that His presence spills into everything, our thoughts, our relationships, our work, our worship. The Christian life is not about containing the Spirit, but about releasing what He has poured in.

Jesus spoke of this in John 7:38. "Out of the believer's heart shall flow rivers of living water." John tells us clearly, He was speaking about the Holy Spirit. The Spirit does not just refresh us. He flows through us. We are meant to be channels, not reservoirs.

So many of us live spiritually dry lives not because the Spirit is absent, but because we've stopped the flow. We receive but we don't pour out. We pray but do not act. We hear but do not obey. The result is stagnation.

But when we cooperate with the Spirit, when we say yes, when we forgive, when we serve, when we step out in faith, the Spirit keeps flowing. He keeps renewing. He keeps transforming not only us but those around us.

This is why the saints had such impact. They were not stronger or more gifted than us. They simply allowed the

Spirit to move through them, unhindered. As St. Catherine of Siena said, "Be who God meant you to be and you will set the world on fire."

If you feel dry, ask not just to be filled, but to be released. Let the Spirit overflow.

Journal Prompt:

In what area of your life have you been holding back what God has poured into you? What would it look like to let the Holy Spirit flow through you today?

"Let anyone who is thirsty come to me, and let the one who believes in me drink. As the scripture has said, 'Out of the believer's heart shall flow rivers of living water.'"
John 7:37–38

Mon 9-1

Prayer:

Holy Spirit, flow through me.

I do not want to keep You for myself.

I want to carry Your presence into the world.

Open my hands, open my heart, open my life to
be a vessel of grace.

Where I have held back, I release control.

Use me to refresh others, to speak hope, to serve
in love, to overflow with joy.

Let my life be evidence that You are alive and at
work in the world.

Father, I ask this in Jesus' name, through the
power of your Holy Spirit.

Amen.

DAY 9 – EMPOWERED FOR MISSION

Devotional Reflection:

Pentecost did not end with a worship service. It began a mission. The Holy Spirit did not come so the disciples could feel spiritually uplifted. He came so they could go. "You will receive power when the Holy Spirit has come upon you; and you will be my witnesses," Jesus said (Acts 1:8).

That is the purpose of the Spirit's power. Not just for personal transformation, but for the mission of the Gospel. The same Spirit who hovered over the waters at creation, who descended like a dove at Jesus' baptism, now empowers you to be a witness in the world.

The Catechism reminds us that "by the power of the Holy Spirit, God's children can bear much fruit" and are "called to the apostolate" (CCC 2013, 2044). That means we are sent, not just clergy or religious, but every baptized person.

Your life may not look like Peter's or Paul's, but your call is no less real. There are people in your life, family, co-workers, friends, who may never walk into a church, but they are watching you. The Spirit sends you to be a light where you are, not where someone else is.

Tues 9-2   31

And you are not sent empty-handed. The Spirit gives power, wisdom, and boldness for whatever your assignment looks like. Whether you speak from a stage or sit at a bedside,

whether you share your story or simply show up in love, the Holy Spirit is with you.

Journal Prompt:

What does it mean for you personally to be a "witness" in your current season of life? Ask the Holy Spirit to show you one way to live that out today.

"You will receive power when the Holy Spirit has come upon you; and you will be my witnesses… to the ends of the earth."
Acts 1:8

Prayer:

Holy Spirit, send me.

Give me eyes to see where You are already at work and feet that are willing to follow.

Give me courage to speak when I need to and love that speaks even when I am silent.

Remind me that I am not on mission alone.

You go with me.

Use my life to reveal Jesus wherever I am planted.

Let my witness be faithful, joyful, and bold.

Father, I ask this in Jesus' name, through the power of your Holy Spirit.

Amen.

DAY 10 – FRUIT THAT LASTS

Devotional Reflection:

One of the surest signs of the Holy Spirit's presence in our lives is lasting fruit. Not just emotional moments but transformed living. Jesus said, "You did not choose me, but I chose you. And I appointed you to go and bear fruit, fruit that will last" (John 15:16).

The fruit of the Spirit, as Paul describes it in Galatians 5, is love, joy, peace, patience, kindness, generosity, faithfulness, gentleness, and self-control. These are not self-improvement goals. They are the result of life lived in surrender to the Spirit.

Many people try hard to be better Christians. But fruit does not come from striving. It comes from abiding. A branch doesn't produce fruit by effort. It produces fruit by staying connected to the vine.

When we invite the Holy Spirit daily and walk in step with Him, He begins to shape us slowly but powerfully. Our reactions change. Our words soften. Our desires shift. The transformation may not always feel dramatic, but it is real.

Others begin to notice it before we do. A little more patience. A little more peace. A little more love. This is not performance. It is presence. The Spirit is alive within us, cultivating the character of Christ.

The most powerful witness to the world may not be what we say, but who we are becoming. Fruit speaks. And when it lasts, it glorifies God.

Journal Prompt:

Which fruit of the Spirit is growing in your life right now? Which one do you feel called to pray for and cultivate more deeply?

"You did not choose me, but I chose you. And I appointed you to go and bear fruit, fruit that will last..."
John 15:16

Wed 9\3

Prayer:

Holy Spirit, grow Your fruit in me.

I cannot love, forgive, or endure in my own strength. I need You.

Shape my heart to look more like Jesus.

Let Your life take root in mine, and let others taste the goodness of Your Spirit in me.

Help me to abide in You, and to trust that You are always at work, even when growth feels slow.

May my life bear fruit that brings glory to the Father.

Father, I ask this in Jesus' name, through the power of your Holy Spirit.

Amen.

DAY 11 – THE SPIRIT WHO COMFORTS

Devotional Reflection:

One of the most personal and beautiful names given to the Holy Spirit is Comforter. Jesus, knowing what His disciples would soon face, the cross, His absence, persecution, promised them this gift: "I will not leave you orphaned" (John 14:18). He knew they would need more than courage. They would need comfort. Not temporary relief, but sustaining peace.

We often think of the Holy Spirit as the One who gives us strength and boldness, and that is true. But Scripture also reveals Him as the One who comes close in our weakness and grief. "The Spirit helps us in our weakness," Paul writes in Romans 8:26, "for we do not know how to pray as we ought, but that very Spirit intercedes with sighs too deep for words."

When we hurt, when life breaks our heart, the Spirit draws near. Not always with answers, but always with presence. That presence is not passive. It is active. He holds us in our sorrow. He carries us through suffering. He gently reminds us we are not alone, not forgotten, not abandoned.

There have been moments in my life where I've prayed and could barely form the words. What I've come to understand is that the Holy Spirit speaks for us when we

Thur 9-4

can't. He turns our silence into prayer and our tears into holy intercession.

St. Teresa of Avila once said, "God withholds Himself from no one who perseveres." If you are in a season of pain, know this: God is not far off. The Spirit is near. Not only to empower you, but to comfort you.

Journal Prompt:

Where in your life do you need the Holy Spirit's comfort right now? Take time to write or pray from that place of need.

"The Spirit helps us in our weakness; for we do not know how to pray as we ought, but that very Spirit intercedes with sighs too deep for words."
Romans 8:26

Prayer:

Holy Spirit, I need Your comfort.

You know the pain I carry and the fears I cannot name.

When words fail me, meet me in the silence.

Intercede on my behalf.

Speak peace into my confusion.

Wrap me in the warmth of Your presence and remind me that I am never alone.

Hold me close, and let Your love be the place I rest today.

Father, I ask this in Jesus' name, through the power of your Holy Spirit.

Amen.

DAY 12 – A NEW BEGINNING

Devotional Reflection:

Pentecost was a beginning, not an ending. It launched the Church into a Spirit-filled, mission-driven future. The beauty of the Holy Spirit is that He continually invites us to begin again. Each new day, each new season, each time we turn our hearts back to God, the Spirit is ready to fill us afresh.

Maybe the last two weeks have stirred something in you. Maybe it's a longing for more of God. Maybe it's a desire to live with greater faith, purpose, and intimacy with the Holy Spirit. Or maybe, even with all we've reflected on, you still feel stuck, unsure how to move forward. The good news is that you do not have to figure it all out first. You simply begin.

The Catechism reminds us that "the Holy Spirit prepares us with His grace, in order to draw us to Christ" (CCC 737). That means we don't begin on our own. We begin by responding to the Spirit already at work within us.

Think of Peter. He denied Jesus three times. He was full of regret and shame. And yet, on the day of Pentecost, it was Peter who stood up and proclaimed the Gospel boldly. What changed? The Holy Spirit gave him a new beginning.

You are never disqualified from what God wants to do in your life. The past does not get the final word. The Spirit does. Wherever you find yourself today, whether on fire or feeling dry, this is your invitation: start again. Invite the Spirit to renew your heart and restore your hope. You are not behind. You are right on time for what God wants to do next.

Journal Prompt:

How has the Holy Spirit stirred your heart during this time? What would it look like to begin again today, fully surrendered and Spirit-filled?

"Therefore, if anyone is in Christ, there is a new creation: everything old has passed away; see, everything has become new!"
2 Corinthians 5:17

Fri 9-5

Prayer:

Holy Spirit, thank You for the gift of new beginnings.

Even when I feel unworthy, You offer me renewal.

I give You my past, my regrets, and all that feels stuck.

Breathe life into what has grown cold and give me the grace to follow You forward.

Make this day a fresh start, a holy offering, a moment where I choose to walk with You again.

Come, Holy Spirit. I am ready.

Father, I ask this in Jesus' name, through the power of your Holy Spirit.

Amen.

DAY 13 – A TIME OF PRAYER: FILLED WITH POWER

Devotional Reflection:

The Holy Spirit does not come to observe. He comes to transform.

Throughout Scripture, we see that when the Spirit fills someone, something changes. Fear gives way to courage. Silence turns into proclamation. Weakness becomes strength. This is not emotional hype, it is the power of God dwelling in a willing heart.

Today is a time not just to reflect, but to respond.

Ask yourself: Have I welcomed the power of the Holy Spirit into every part of my life? Or am I holding back areas I think I must manage on my own?

Being filled with the Spirit is not a one-time moment. It is a way of living, a posture of daily surrender and openness. The Spirit comes to empower you in your calling, to strengthen you in your weakness, and to use your life to bless others. But He waits for the invitation.

Today, in the quiet, ask for that filling again. Not just for strength, but for transformation. The same Spirit who filled the disciples at Pentecost is ready to fill you.

You don't have to feel powerful to receive. You only need to be open. Say with your heart, "Holy Spirit, fill me with power." Then wait. Expect. Trust. He comes where He is invited.

Prayer Focus:

Sit in a posture of surrender, hands open, heart ready. Pray this:

Holy Spirit, I receive Your power. Fill every part of me. Use my life for Your glory.

Pray for boldness, clarity, healing, and renewed fire to live for Christ.

"You will receive power when the Holy Spirit has come upon you; and you will be my witnesses."
Acts 1:8

Closing Prayer:

Holy Spirit, fill me again.

Not just with emotion, but with power.

Let Your strength rise in my weakness, Your courage in my fear, Your voice in my silence.

I am ready. I am willing.

Fill me and send me.

Father, I ask this in Jesus' name, through the power of your Holy Spirit.

Amen.

DAY 14: GO DEEPER ON SUNDAYS

You can watch this week's message at [BruceDownes.org]

Sat 9-4

How to **GROW** the **FRUITS** of the *Holy Spirit*

INTRODUCTION

The Holy Spirit doesn't only empower us. He transforms us. His presence bears fruit in us, not just momentary inspiration, but lasting change. Love, joy, peace, patience, kindness, generosity, faithfulness, gentleness, and self-control, these are not personality traits. They are signs of the Spirit at work.

This theme is about spiritual maturity. It's about the slow, steady growth of Christlike character. And just like fruit on a tree, it takes time, attention, and a willingness to let God do the pruning.

Each day, we'll focus on one aspect of the Spirit's fruit. You'll be invited not to try harder, but to abide deeper. To let the Spirit form in you what you cannot produce on your own.

God's goal is not simply to use you, but to make you whole. Let this be a season of inner renewal, as the Spirit cultivates something beautiful in your life.

Mon. 9-8

DAY 1 – THE ONE FRUIT OF THE SPIRIT

Devotional Reflection:

When we think of the fruit of the Holy Spirit, it's easy to picture a basket of individual virtues, love, joy, peace, and so on, as though they are separate items we can pick and choose. But in Galatians 5, St. Paul doesn't write "fruits of the Spirit are." He says, "The fruit of the Spirit is" singular. One fruit. Many expressions.

This matters more than we might realize. The fruit of the Spirit isn't a list of behaviors to strive for one at a time. It's the result of a life being transformed by the Holy Spirit from within. When we stay connected to God, He produces in us a fruit that looks like Jesus, love, joy, peace, patience, kindness, generosity, faithfulness, gentleness, and self-control, all together, not in isolation.

Jesus made this clear in John 15:5: "I am the vine, you are the branches. Those who abide in me and I in them bear much fruit." The fruit comes not from trying harder, but from abiding deeper. A healthy branch doesn't force fruit to appear. It stays attached to the vine, and the fruit comes naturally.

So, it is with us. If we want to grow the fruit of the Spirit, our first priority isn't to become more patient or kinder by effort alone. It's to stay close to Jesus. The more we invite the Holy

Spirit into our daily lives, the more we'll find this fruit beginning to grow, often slowly, quietly, and steadily.

This kind of fruit lasts. It nourishes others. It glorifies God. And it becomes a living witness to the Spirit's presence in us. The question is not, "Am I working hard enough?" The real question is, "Am I staying connected to the source?"

Journal Prompt:

Which part of the fruit of the Spirit feels most present in your life right now? Which feels most lacking? Bring both to prayer today.

"The fruit of the Spirit is love, joy, peace, patience, kindness, generosity, faithfulness, gentleness, and self-control."
Galatians 5:22–23

Prayer:

Holy Spirit, I want to bear fruit that lasts.

Help me to stay rooted in You today.

Grow in me the character of Jesus, each part of this one fruit in harmony.

I give You permission to work in me, to change me gently from the inside out.

Let my life reflect Your presence through the fruit that only You can produce.

Father, I ask this in Jesus' name, through the power of your Holy Spirit.

Amen.

DAY 2 – LOVE COMES FIRST

Devotional Reflection:

Of all the fruit the Holy Spirit grows in our lives, love is named first, and that is no accident. St. Paul isn't just listing virtues randomly. Love is foundational. Without love, all the other fruits lose their depth. Joy becomes shallow. Patience becomes pride. Even generosity can become performance if love isn't the root.

The Catechism tells us, "Charity is the soul of the holiness to which all are called" (CCC 826). This love, agape love, is more than emotion or affection. It is self-giving, sacrificial, and wholly centered on the good of the other. It's the love Jesus poured out on the Cross and continues to pour into our hearts through the Holy Spirit.

Romans 5:5 says, "God's love has been poured into our hearts through the Holy Spirit." That means we are not expected to manufacture this kind of love on our own. It is not about trying harder. It is about receiving more deeply. The Spirit gives us access to divine love, and as we grow in that love, the other fruits follow.

It's easy to love people who love us back. But what about those who annoy us, wound us, or make life hard? That's where the Spirit does His deepest work. I've seen that kind of love expressed in quiet moments, through

Tues 9-9-25

people who forgive when no one expects it, who serve when they're tired, or who bless others with no thought of reward.

This love is not natural. It's supernatural. And it is the mark of a Spirit-filled life. If you are struggling to love someone today, ask the Holy Spirit to love through you. He will. The fruit always starts with love, and from there, everything grows.

Journal Prompt:

Who in your life is difficult to love right now? Ask the Holy Spirit for grace to love them with Christ's heart, not your own.

"God's love has been poured into our hearts through the Holy Spirit that has been given to us."
Romans 5:5

Prayer:

Holy Spirit, teach me how to love as You love.

Not just when it's easy, but when it's hard.

Pour into my heart the love of Christ, selfless, generous, forgiving, and kind.

Let that love shape how I speak, how I listen, how I respond.

May others see not just me, but the love of Jesus growing in me.

Father, I ask this in Jesus' name, through the power of your Holy Spirit.

Amen.

DAY 3 – JOY THAT REMAINS

Devotional Reflection:

Joy is often misunderstood. We confuse it with happiness, a passing feeling that comes when things go our way. But true joy is not tied to circumstances. It doesn't fade when life is hard. Joy is a fruit of the Spirit, which means it comes from God, not from our environment.

Nehemiah told the people of Israel, "The joy of the Lord is your strength" (Nehemiah 8:10). Not the joy of your achievements or circumstances, but the joy that flows from knowing the Lord. This joy is deeply rooted in the presence and promises of God.

In Acts 16, we see Paul and Silas beaten and imprisoned for preaching the Gospel. What did they do? They sang hymns of praise. Not because they enjoyed the pain, but because they had a joy that could not be taken away. That kind of joy isn't manufactured. It's the work of the Spirit.

Sometimes joy is loud and full of laughter. Other times it's quiet, a steady peace that says, "God is here, and I am His."

It's not about forcing positivity. It's about trusting God in every circumstance.

I've known people who carried enormous burdens and still radiated peace and joy. What was their secret? It wasn't that life was easy. It was that they had learned to lean into the Holy Spirit, letting His presence comfort them, guide them, and fill them in places the world could never reach.

Today, let the Spirit remind you that joy isn't the absence of hardship. It's the presence of Christ within it.

If you feel joyless today, ask the Holy Spirit to awaken joy in your heart, not by changing everything around you, but by meeting you where you are. That is the kind of joy that remains.

Journal Prompt:

Where have you lost your sense of joy? Ask the Holy Spirit to restore it, not based on your situation, but on His presence within you.

"As the Father has loved me, so I have loved you; abide in my love... I have said these things to you so that my joy may be in you, and that your joy may be complete."
John 15:9, 11

Wed 9-10

Prayer:

Holy Spirit, restore my joy today.

Not a fleeting emotion, but a deep, steady
strength rooted in Your presence.

Help me to rejoice in all seasons, not because life
is easy, but because You are near.

Let my joy be a witness that You are real, faithful,
and good.

Even in struggle, I choose to praise You.

Father, I ask this in Jesus' name, through the
power of your Holy Spirit.

Amen.

DAY 4 – PEACE BEYOND UNDERSTANDING

Devotional Reflection:

Peace is one of the most treasured gifts in life, yet often the most elusive. We search for it in rest, in achievement, in relationships, and sometimes in simply trying to escape life's pressures. But the kind of peace the Holy Spirit offers isn't based on external calm or the absence of stress. It's deeper. It's internal. It is the presence of God, steadying us even when everything around us feels uncertain.

Jesus promised this peace to His disciples as He prepared to leave them. "Peace I leave with you; my peace I give to you," He said in John 14:27. "I do not give to you as the world gives. Do not let your hearts be troubled, and do not let them be afraid." He wasn't talking about shallow reassurance. He was promising the indwelling presence of the Holy Spirit, God with us and in us, our Comforter.

This peace is not something we earn or produce. It's a fruit of the Spirit. It grows in us over time, especially in the places where we feel stretched or anxious. I've come to realize that the Spirit often grows peace most deeply when I slow down long enough to truly be still before

Thurs
9-11

God, not to fix things, not even to understand, but simply to rest in His nearness.

The Catechism teaches that peace is "the tranquility of order" (CCC 2304), a harmony that comes when our hearts align with God's will. This kind of peace guards our minds. It allows us to respond to life, not react to it. It becomes a quiet anchor within us that holds firm when the waves rise.

Today, invite the Holy Spirit to plant that kind of peace in you. Not a fleeting feeling, but a deep-rooted awareness that God is with you, right now, right here.

Journal Prompt:

What's disrupting your peace right now? Ask the Holy Spirit to meet you there and bring calm that doesn't depend on outcomes.

"Peace I leave with you; my peace I give to you. I do not give to you as the world gives."
John 14:27

Prayer:

Holy Spirit, I need Your peace today.

Still the voices of worry and fear within me.

Anchor me in the presence of Jesus and calm my
anxious thoughts.

Help me to trust what I cannot yet see and to rest
in Your love.

Let Your peace guard my heart, shape my words
and carry me through this day.

Holy Spirit, fill me now.

Father, I ask this in Jesus' name, through the
power of your Holy Spirit.

Amen.

DAY 5 – PATIENCE IN THE PROCESS

Devotional Reflection:

Few things test our faith like waiting. We want results. We want resolution. And we want them now. But God rarely works on our timetable. He forms us in the waiting. That's why patience is one of the most vital, and most difficult, fruits of the Holy Spirit.

Patience isn't just about enduring delay. It's about trusting that God is at work, even when we can't see movement. Paul writes in Romans 8:25, "If we hope for what we do not see, we wait for it with patience." This is hope-filled waiting. Waiting that leans into God instead of turning away.

I've often found that the seasons when I've grown most spiritually weren't the ones filled with breakthroughs or answers, but the times when I had to cling to God with empty hands. When prayers seemed unanswered, and progress felt slow. And yet, the Spirit was doing deep work in my heart, strengthening my faith, softening my pride, and teaching me how to surrender.

The saints understood this well. St. Francis de Sales advised, "Have patience with all things, but chiefly have patience with yourself." The Spirit's work in us is a lifelong journey, not a sprint. He is not in a hurry. He is forming the image of Christ within us, and that takes time.

If you're in a waiting season, waiting for healing, direction, provision, or the return of someone you love, know this: the waiting is not wasted. God is working. You are being shaped. Stay connected to the Spirit. Lean into grace. And trust that, in time, fruit will come.

Journal Prompt:

What are you waiting for right now? How is the Holy Spirit inviting you to trust rather than rush?

"But if we hope for what we do not see, we wait for it with patience."
Romans 8:25

Sat. 9-13

Prayer:

Holy Spirit, grow patience in me today.

I surrender my timeline, my frustration, and my fear.

Help me to trust Your unseen work, even when answers seem far away.

Give me grace to wait with hope and strength to persevere.

Remind me that You are always faithful and that You waste nothing.

Form me in the process and deepen my trust in You.

Father, I ask this in Jesus' name, through the power of your Holy Spirit.

Amen.

DAY 6 - A TIME OF PRAYER: LET THE FRUIT GROW

Devotional Reflection:

This past week, we've walked through what it means to grow in the fruits of the Holy Spirit, love, joy, peace, patience, kindness, and more. These are not things we force. They are the evidence of a life surrendered to the Spirit.

But today is not about examining your growth. It's about sitting with the Gardener.

The fruit of the Spirit grows slowly. Quietly. Often unnoticed. And yet, God is always at work beneath the surface. The Spirit does not rush the process. He tends to it. He waters. He prunes. He waits. And He invites us to do the same.

So today, resist the temptation to evaluate yourself. Just rest. Rest in the truth that God is at work in you, even when you can't see it. Rest in the love of the Father, the grace of the Son, and the presence of the Holy Spirit.

Say this as you begin your time of prayer:
Holy Spirit, grow Your fruit in me.
Then be still. Listen. Let the Spirit remind you of His patience. Let Him speak into your weariness. Let Him show you how He's already changing your heart.

Fruit grows when it remains connected to the vine. Today, simply remain.

Prayer Focus:

Pray with this question:
Holy Spirit, what are You growing in me?
Wait in silence. Trust what He reveals. Pray for the fruit of the Spirit to increase in your life and to bless those around you.

"The fruit of the Spirit is love, joy, peace, patience, kindness, generosity, faithfulness, gentleness, and self-control."
Galatians 5:22–23

Closing Prayer:

Holy Spirit, I pause with You today.

No striving, no proving, just presence.

I offer You the soil of my heart.

Grow what You will. Prune what You must.

Let the fruit of my life reflect the love and character of Jesus.

I remain in You.

Father, I ask this in Jesus' name, through the power of your Holy Spirit.

Amen.

DAY 7: GO DEEPER ON SUNDAYS

You can watch this week's message at [BruceDownes.org]

DAY 8 – KINDNESS THAT CHANGES EVERYTHING

Devotional Reflection:

Kindness is more than just being polite. It is a spiritual strength, a fruit of the Holy Spirit that reflects the mercy and goodness of God to a hurting world. In a culture that often celebrates harshness or sarcasm, kindness stands out as radical. It speaks of a different kingdom. A different King.

Paul writes in Ephesians 4:32, "Be kind to one another, tenderhearted, forgiving one another, as God in Christ has forgiven you." This kind of kindness costs something. It often requires us to go against our instinct to defend, to withdraw, or to judge. But it's in these moments that the Holy Spirit offers to grow something different in us, compassion that acts, gentleness that sees, and mercy that reflects Christ.

I've seen lives changed through simple acts of kindness, a conversation when someone felt invisible, a warm smile in a moment of shame, a meal delivered at just the right time. The Holy Spirit uses these small gestures to whisper the love of God into people's lives.

Kindness can be especially hard when we're tired or hurting. That's when we ask the Spirit to be strong in us.

He doesn't just grow kindness when it's convenient, He grows it in us when we surrender. When we say, "Holy Spirit, love through me."

St. Teresa of Calcutta said, "Kind words can be short and easy to speak, but their echoes are truly endless." Today, ask the Holy Spirit to use you. To soften your words. To guide your responses. To give you eyes to see someone who needs a glimpse of God's kindness through you.

Journal Prompt:

Where in your day do you most often forget to be kind? Invite the Holy Spirit into that space with intention.

"Be kind to one another, tenderhearted, forgiving one another, as God in Christ has forgiven you."
Ephesians 4:32

Prayer:

Holy Spirit, grow kindness in me today.

In my thoughts, in my words, in my reactions, let me reflect Your love.

Help me to be tenderhearted, even when it's easier to be indifferent.

Remind me of how gently You've treated me, so I may do the same for others.

Let my kindness be a doorway for others to experience Your goodness.

Work through me in every small act of grace.

Father, I ask this in Jesus' name, through the power of your Holy Spirit.

Amen.

DAY 9 – GENEROSITY THAT FLOWS FROM GRACE

Devotional Reflection:

When we think of generosity, we often think of giving money or possessions. But the fruit of the Spirit called generosity goes much deeper. It's not just about what we give, it's about how we live. A generous life flows from a heart that knows it has received much and therefore delights in giving freely.

In Acts 2, after Pentecost, the Holy Spirit moved powerfully, and the first believers began sharing everything they had. "All who believed were together and had all things in common… they gave to each as any had need" (Acts 2:44–45). They didn't give because someone told them to. They gave because they were so full of God's love that it naturally spilled over.

That's what happens when the Spirit lives in us. Our hearts open. Our hands loosen. We no longer ask, "How much do I have to give?" Instead, we ask, "How can I bless?" Whether it's our time, our attention, our skills, our resources, or our kindness, the Spirit nudges us to be generous in ways both big and small.

One of the most generous people I've ever met had very little materially. But they always made space for others, always had time, always gave encouragement. That kind

Wed 9-17

of generosity cannot be taught. It's the fruit of the Holy Spirit alive in someone's life.

And here's the miracle: generosity doesn't deplete us. It multiplies. As we pour out, the Spirit fills us again. We're not giving from lack. We're giving from overflow.

Ask the Holy Spirit today: "Where can I be more generous?" And then respond, not out of obligation, but from the grace you've already received.

Journal Prompt:

Where is God prompting you to live more generously? How can you reflect His abundant heart today?

"All who believed were together and had all things in common… they would sell their possessions and goods and distribute the proceeds to all, as any had need."
Acts 2:44–45

Prayer:

Holy Spirit, open my heart to live generously.

Teach me to give freely, not just from my resources but from my life.

Let generosity become my lifestyle, a daily response to Your grace.

Make me aware of needs around me and willing to act in love.

Help me reflect Your abundance in the way I give and serve.

May my generosity open the door for others to see You.

Father, I ask this in Jesus' name, through the power of your Holy Spirit.

Amen.

DAY 10 – FAITHFULNESS IN THE EVERYDAY

Devotional Reflection:

Faithfulness often doesn't feel exciting. It's not loud or flashy. It's made up of steady steps, quiet prayers, consistent service, and small acts of obedience. But in God's eyes, faithfulness is powerful. It's fruit that proves our roots are deep in Him.

The Holy Spirit produces this fruit in our lives over time, when we keep showing up, keep trusting, keep saying yes, even when no one notices. Lamentations 3:22–23 tells us, "The steadfast love of the Lord never ceases... great is your faithfulness." God Himself is our model of faithfulness. He never fails, never forgets, never abandons.

The more we walk with the Spirit, the more we begin to reflect that same faithfulness. I've seen it in parents loving through exhaustion, in friends walking through difficult seasons, in people who keep praying when they see no results. That quiet strength, the decision to stay the course, is a beautiful witness.

Sometimes we think of faithfulness as big commitments, but more often it's lived out in the small things. In keeping your word. In praying when no one else knows.

In forgiving again. In trusting God when the way forward isn't clear.

The world rewards quick results and visible success. But God sees the long obedience. The perseverance. The heart that says, "I'm still here, Lord. I'm still yours." The Holy Spirit strengthens us to live like that, to be dependable in a world full of distraction.

Today, ask the Spirit to grow faithfulness in your life. Not perfection, but consistency. Not applause, but deep, steady trust.

Journal Prompt:

Where is God calling you to stay faithful right now, even if you feel unseen or tired?

_____

"His mercies never come to an end; they are new every morning; great is your faithfulness."
Lamentations 3:22–23

_____

PRAYER:

Holy Spirit, make me faithful.

Teach me to serve You in the ordinary, the quiet, the hidden places.

Give me strength to keep going when I feel weary or unnoticed.

Let my life reflect the trustworthiness of Your love.

Make me steady in my commitments, patient in my journey and rooted in grace.

I want to be found faithful in Your eyes.

Father, I ask this in Jesus' name, through the power of your Holy Spirit.

Amen.

DAY 11 – GENTLENESS WITH STRENGTH

Devotional Reflection:

Gentleness is one of the most misunderstood qualities in our culture. We often think of it as softness, even weakness. But the gentleness that comes from the Holy Spirit is far from fragile. It is strength under control, love that chooses compassion over harshness, humility over pride.

In Philippians 4:5, Paul writes, "Let your gentleness be known to everyone. The Lord is near." Why does this matter? Because the presence of God changes how we treat others. When we know He is near, we no longer need to dominate, defend, or prove ourselves. We can respond with calm, not control.

Jesus Himself described His heart as "gentle and humble" (Matthew 11:29). He had the power to calm storms, cast out demons, and command angels. Yet He stooped low to wash feet. He welcomed children. He restored the fallen with tenderness. That is the strength of the Spirit-filled life.

Gentleness shows up in how we speak, how we listen, and how we respond, especially under pressure. I've seen its power in moments where someone could have lashed out but chose to pause and speak with grace. That kind of self-restraint doesn't come naturally. It comes from walking closely with the Holy Spirit.

As the Spirit transforms us, He gives us a different kind of power, not to push others down but to lift them up. Not to prove we're right, but to draw others near. In a world hungry for peace, gentleness is revolutionary.

Ask the Holy Spirit to shape this fruit in you, not to make you passive, but to make you powerful in love.

Journal Prompt:

Where is the Spirit inviting you to be more gentle, with yourself, with others, or in a specific situation?

_____

"Let your gentleness be known to everyone. The Lord is near."
Philippians 4:5

_____

Prayer:

Holy Spirit, shape my heart to be gentle like
Yours.

Give me strength to speak with love and respond
with kindness.

Teach me to lead with grace, to listen with
humility, and to correct with compassion.

Let Your gentleness take root in me and be
visible in every interaction.

I want others to experience Your nearness
through the way I treat them.

Father, I ask this in Jesus' name, through the
power of your Holy Spirit.

Amen.

DAY 12 – SELF-CONTROL THAT FREES

Devotional Reflection:

Self-control may be the final fruit listed in Galatians 5, but it's the one that holds so much together. Without it, love becomes self-seeking, joy becomes indulgence, and faithfulness fades into convenience. Self-control is what empowers us to choose God's way over our own desires, and that's real freedom.

In Titus 2:11–12, Paul says that the grace of God "trains us… to live lives that are self-controlled, upright, and godly." That word, trains, is important. Self-control isn't instant. It's learned. It's shaped. And it's the Holy Spirit who trains us, not through guilt, but through grace.

I've learned that self-control is not about rigid willpower. It's about yielding. It's about inviting the Spirit into the small moments where we decide who's really in charge. In our reactions. In our appetites. In our schedules. In our thought life.

There have been seasons in my life where I've let impulse lead, and I've seen the damage it can do. But I've also seen the joy and peace that comes when I let the Spirit lead. When I choose discipline over distraction, purpose over comfort, grace overindulgence.

Self-control is not about suppressing desire. It's about learning to desire what is best. It's about choosing what gives life, not just what feels good. And every time we make that choice with the Spirit's help, something inside us grows stronger.

Today, ask the Holy Spirit to train you, to shape your choices, your cravings, your responses. Let Him lead you into true freedom: the freedom of a life under the gentle control of God.

Journal Prompt:

Where in your life do you struggle to walk in self-control? How might the Spirit help you choose differently today?

"Live lives that are self-controlled, upright, and godly."
Titus 2:12

Prayer:

Holy Spirit, I give You control.

Lead me in the choices that honor You, even when they're hard.

Teach me to say no when I need to, and yes to what leads to life.

Help me grow strong in spirit and steady in purpose.

Let Your grace shape every area of my life.

I want to live free, not driven by impulse, but led by love.

Father, I ask this in Jesus' name, through the power of your Holy Spirit.

Amen.

DAY 13 - A TIME OF PRAYER: ROOTED AND GROWING

Devotional Reflection:

Spiritual fruit doesn't grow in a hurry. It grows through abiding, day by day, choice by choice, surrender by surrender. As we end this week reflecting on the fruits of the Holy Spirit, let's not rush to results. Let's return to the root.

Jesus said, "Abide in me as I abide in you… Those who abide in me and I in them bear much fruit" (John 15:4–5). The Spirit cultivates fruit in us not through our striving, but through our remaining. Remaining in God's love. Remaining in His Word. Remaining when we feel dry, distracted, or discouraged.

You may not see the change right away. But the Spirit is at work. Even in silence. Even when you feel nothing. The fruit is growing.

So today, don't measure your progress. Rest in the presence of the Gardener. Let the Holy Spirit water the places you've surrendered. Let Him breathe peace over the parts that feel slow.

You are being shaped more than you know.

Prayer Focus:

Pray with these words:

Holy Spirit, I abide in You. Keep me rooted. Keep me steady. Grow fruit in me that will last.

Ask for patience in the process and fresh joy in the journey.

"Those who abide in me and I in them bear much fruit."
John 15:5

Closing Prayer:

Holy Spirit, I give You the soil of my life.

Let Your fruit grow in me, not for my sake but for Your glory.

Teach me to remain in Your love when I cannot see results.

Help me to trust the slow work of God.

I am rooted in You.

Father, I ask this in Jesus' name, through the power of your Holy Spirit.

Amen.

DAY 14: GO DEEPER ON SUNDAYS

You can watch this week's message at [BruceDownes.org]

The TRINITY
and the
Holy Spirit

INTRODUCTION

At the very center of our faith is not an idea, but a relationship. One God in three Persons, Father, Son, and Holy Spirit. The Trinity is not just a mystery to be studied. It is a reality to be lived. You were created by the Father, redeemed by the Son, and are now filled with the Spirit.

This theme draws us into communion. Over fourteen days, you'll explore how the Spirit reveals the Son, how He leads us to the Father, and how we are drawn into the very life of God.

The Catechism says that the ultimate purpose of our life is to be united with the Trinity. This is not abstract theology. This is daily life. When we pray, when we listen, when we love, we are invited into divine relationship.

As you reflect, let yourself be drawn deeper into that eternal love. You are not just called to follow God. You are called to live in Him.

DAY 1 – ONE GOD, THREE PERSONS

Devotional Reflection:

The Trinity is one of the most profound mysteries of our faith. We believe in one God, Father, Son, and Holy Spirit. Not three gods. One. And yet, each Person is distinct, fully God, fully present. It's a mystery we cannot fully comprehend, but one we are invited to enter into.

The Catechism teaches that "the Trinity is the central mystery of Christian faith and life... the source of all the other mysteries of faith" (CCC 234). That means we don't believe in the Trinity as an abstract idea. We encounter the Trinity as the living God who invites us into relationship.

Think about it: God the Father created you. God the Son died for you. And God the Holy Spirit lives in you. You were made by the love of the Trinity, redeemed by the love of the Trinity, and now filled with that love. The Holy Spirit doesn't operate separately from the Father and the Son, He reveals them. He draws us into their perfect communion of love.

When Jesus promised the Holy Spirit to His disciples, He said, "I will ask the Father, and he will give you another Advocate... the Spirit of truth... he will take what is mine and declare it to you" (John 14:16–17;

16:14). The Spirit does not speak on His own. He leads us deeper into Christ, and through Christ, to the Father.

The more we walk with the Spirit, the more we come to know the Father's heart and the Son's grace. We begin to live not just as servants of God, but as sons and daughters, drawn into the divine family of love.

Today, pause and thank God for the gift of this mystery. Ask the Spirit to help you live in communion with the Father and the Son.

Journal Prompt:

What part of your relationship with God - Father, Son, or Holy Spirit - do you feel drawn to grow deeper in right now?

"I will ask the Father, and he will give you another Advocate… He will glorify me, because he will take what is mine and declare it to you."
John 14:16, 16:14

Prayer:

Holy Spirit, draw me deeper into the love of the Trinity.

Help me to know the Father's goodness, the Son's mercy, and Your constant presence.

Let me live each day rooted in divine relationship.

Shape my heart to reflect the unity, peace, and love of the God who made me.

Father, Son, and Holy Spirit, You are one, and I am Yours.

Father, I ask this in Jesus' name, through the power of your Holy Spirit.

Amen.

DAY 2 – THE SPIRIT REVEALS THE SON

Devotional Reflection:

One of the primary roles of the Holy Spirit is to reveal Jesus. That might surprise us. We often think of the Spirit in terms of power, presence, or gifts, and rightly so. But the Spirit's greatest desire is to glorify Christ and make Him known to us in a personal, life-changing way.

In John 16:13–14, Jesus said, "When the Spirit of truth comes… He will glorify me, because he will take what is mine and declare it to you." The Spirit is not here to point to Himself. He is here to point us to Jesus. To make Christ real to us, not just historically, but presently, powerfully, personally.

The Catechism tells us that "no one can say 'Jesus is Lord' except by the Holy Spirit" (CCC 152). That means even our faith in Jesus begins with the Spirit's work within us. Without Him, Jesus remains a concept. With Him, Jesus becomes our Savior, our Friend, our Lord.

I've experienced this many times in prayer, when Scripture comes alive in a new way, when I'm convicted of truth, or when I sense Jesus speaking to my heart. That's not imagination. That's the Spirit doing what He does best: revealing the Son.

89

If you ever feel distant from Jesus, don't be discouraged. Invite the Holy Spirit to draw you near. Ask Him to open your heart to the presence of Christ. He will. Because that's His joy, to lead you into intimacy with the Son.

And the more we know Jesus, the more we see the heart of the Father. This is the beauty of the Trinity: each Person reveals the other. It's not theology, it's relationship.

Journal Prompt:

In what area of your life do you need to see Jesus more clearly? Ask the Holy Spirit to reveal Him to you today.

"When the Spirit of truth comes, he will guide you into all the truth… He will glorify me, because he will take what is mine and declare it to you."
John 16:13–14

Prayer:

Holy Spirit, help me see Jesus more clearly.

Open the eyes of my heart to know Him not just with my mind, but with my whole being.

Reveal His mercy, His love, His truth to me in a deeper way.

Let my life be shaped by the One who gave His life for me.

Lead me into deeper friendship with Jesus today.

Father, I ask this in Jesus' name, through the power of your Holy Spirit.

Amen.

DAY 3 – THE SPIRIT UNITES US WITH THE FATHER

Devotional Reflection:

The Spirit not only reveals Jesus, He also draws us into relationship with the Father. It's easy to think of God the Father as distant or hard to reach, especially if we've known earthly fathers who struggled to love well. But the Holy Spirit brings the Father's love close. He teaches us what it means to live as beloved sons and daughters.

In Romans 8:15–16, Paul writes, "You have received a spirit of adoption. When we cry, 'Abba! Father!' it is that very Spirit bearing witness with our spirit that we are children of God." It is the Spirit who teaches us to pray, not just to a far-off God, but to a Father who knows us by name.

The Catechism says the Holy Spirit "makes us live in the communion of love of the Blessed Trinity" (CCC 733). In other words, the Spirit is the One who invites us into the very life of God, Father, Son, and Holy Spirit. We don't observe the Trinity from the outside. We are welcomed into the circle of love.

There are days when I've felt alone or unsure. But I've also known moments of quiet prayer when the Spirit whispers, "You belong. You're not abandoned. You are loved." That assurance doesn't come from ourselves. It comes from the Spirit. And it changes everything.

You are not just someone God tolerates. You are someone the Father delights in. And it is the Spirit who enables you to live from that truth, secure, accepted, known.

Let the Spirit remind you today that you are a child of God. Not one day. Not when you're better. Now.

Journal Prompt:

How do you relate to God the Father? Ask the Holy Spirit to help you experience the Father's love more deeply today.

"When we cry, 'Abba! Father!' it is that very Spirit bearing witness with our spirit that we are children of God." Romans 8:15–16

Prayer:

Holy Spirit, remind me that I am a child of God.

Break down every lie that says I'm unwanted or unloved.

Lead me to the Father's heart, where I am known, accepted, and safe.

Let me live not for approval, but from the truth that I already belong.

Abba, Father, I come to You through the Spirit You've given me.

Father, I ask this in Jesus' name, through the power of your Holy Spirit.

Amen.

DAY 4 – THE SPIRIT IS THE GIFT OF THE TRINITY

Devotional Reflection:

Sometimes we think of the Holy Spirit as a helper sent after Jesus. But from the beginning, the Spirit has been part of the eternal love between the Father and the Son. That love isn't just something God gives. It's Someone. And that Someone now lives in us.

At Pentecost, the Church received the Holy Spirit as a gift not only of power, but of communion. "God's love has been poured into our hearts through the Holy Spirit that has been given to us" (Romans 5:5). This isn't symbolic. It's real. The Spirit brings the very life of the Trinity into our lives.

That means you are never alone. The Spirit is not a visitor. He is the presence of God within you, continually reminding you who you are and whose you are. He empowers you to love when it's hard, to forgive when it hurts, to hope when it's dark. He forms Christ in you and draws you into the Father's embrace.

In moments of quiet prayer, I've sensed this reality so clearly, that I'm being held not by a vague sense of peace, but by the living presence of God Himself. The Spirit is not an accessory to our faith. He is the heartbeat of it.

As you go through today, remember you carry the gift of the Trinity within you. The Spirit doesn't just visit on holy days or in church buildings. He is with you at the kitchen sink, in traffic, during meetings, in moments of joy and in your tears.

Journal Prompt:

What does it mean to you that God's love has been poured into your heart through the Holy Spirit? Sit with that truth today.

---

*"God's love has been poured into our hearts
through the Holy Spirit that has
been given to us."*
Romans 5:5

Prayer:

Holy Spirit, thank You for being the gift of the Father and the Son.

Let me never take for granted that You live within me.

Fill me again with the love that flows between the Father and the Son.

Make me more aware of Your presence today in the stillness and in the noise.

Let Your love flow through my words, my actions, and my thoughts.

Father, I ask this in Jesus' name, through the power of your Holy Spirit.

Amen.

DAY 5 – CREATED BY THE FATHER, REDEEMED BY THE SON, FILLED WITH THE SPIRIT

Devotional Reflection:

The Trinity isn't just a theological concept,it's the pattern of our salvation. Everything we believe and everything we are flows from this divine relationship. You were created by the Father, redeemed by the Son, and now filled with the Spirit.

The Catechism says, "The whole divine economy is the common work of the three divine persons" (CCC 258). That means the Father, Son, and Holy Spirit are not doing separate jobs. They are united in one great mission: to draw us into the life of God.

The Father created you in love. He saw you before time began. His plan has always been to bring you into communion with Himself.

The Son came to rescue you. Jesus became one of us, not to condemn, but to save. On the Cross, He bore our sin, healed our brokenness, and made a way back to the Father.

And the Holy Spirit now lives within you, breathing divine life into your everyday moments. He empowers you to live as a child of God, not just believing in Him, but walking with Him.

I've found that when I pray with this understanding, when I say "Thank You, Father," "Help me, Jesus," "Fill me, Holy Spirit," something shifts in my soul. I don't feel like I'm praying to a far-off God. I feel like I'm being drawn into a divine family. And that's exactly what the Trinity is: a communion of love into which we are welcomed.

You were made for this. Not just to know about God, but to know Him in His fullness. Let the Trinity shape how you pray, how you think, and how you live.

Journal Prompt:

What does it mean to you personally to be created by the Father, redeemed by the Son, and filled with the Holy Spirit?

_____

"For through him [Christ] both of us have
access in one Spirit to the Father."
Ephesians 2:18

_____

Prayer:

Father, thank You for creating me in love.

Jesus, thank You for redeeming me at such a cost.

Holy Spirit, thank You for filling me and leading me each day.

Draw me into the life of the Trinity, and let my life reflect the unity and love that exists in You.

Help me to live from that divine relationship, not just believing but belonging.

Father, I ask this in Jesus' name, through the power of your Holy Spirit.

Amen.

DAY 6 - A TIME OF PRAYER: DWELLING IN THE TRINITY

Devotional Reflection:

The mystery of the Trinity is not meant to confuse us. It is meant to welcome us. One God in three Persons - Father, Son, and Holy Spirit - has invited us into divine communion. That means the life of God is not distant. It is our home.

In prayer, we often address God without considering that the entire Trinity is present. The Father receives us in love. The Son intercedes for us in grace. The Spirit helps us cry, "Abba, Father." We do not stand outside the circle. We are drawn inside.

The Catechism says, "God's innermost secret is that God himself is an eternal exchange of love... and he has destined us to share in that exchange" (CCC 221). That is what prayer is. That is what your life is becoming.

Today, take time to simply dwell in that truth. Let yourself be loved. Let yourself be held in the life of the Trinity.

Don't strive. Just remain.

Prayer Focus:

Pray with this phrase:

sat 9-31

Father, Son, and Spirit, I am Yours. Let me live in Your love.

Rest in stillness. Allow the love of God to surround you and fill you.

"May they also be in us... that the world may believe that you have sent me."
John 17:21

Closing Prayer:

Father, Son, and Holy Spirit,

Draw me into Your love.

Let me rest in Your unity, find joy in Your presence,

and live from the strength of being held by You.

I do not need to understand it all. I simply say yes.

I am Yours.

Father, I ask this in Jesus' name, through the power of your Holy Spirit.

Amen.

DAY 7: GO DEEPER ON SUNDAYS

You can watch this week's message at [BruceDownes.org]

DAY 8 – MADE IN THE IMAGE OF THE TRINITY

Devotional Reflection:

Scripture tells us that we are made in the image and likeness of God (Genesis 1:27). But what does that really mean? It means we are made not only with dignity and purpose, but also for relationship. Because God is a communion of persons - Father, Son, and Holy Spirit - we, too, are created for communion.

The Catechism teaches that "being in the image of God, the human individual possesses the dignity of a person... able to enter into communion with others and with God" (CCC 357). In other words, our capacity for love, relationship, creativity, and spiritual hunger is not random. It reflects the Trinity.

God is not a solitary being. From all eternity, the Father loves the Son, the Son loves the Father, and the Spirit is that love poured out. And we, created in that image, are made to give and receive love. To be known and to know. To live not in isolation, but in community.

I've learned that when I'm most disconnected from others or from God, I'm also the most restless. But when I lean into relationship, when I forgive, when I open my heart, when I spend time in prayer, something in me feels whole again. That's not coincidence. That's design.

You were made to live in communion. First with God, and then with others. If you're feeling alone today, the Spirit can remind you who you are and draw you back into connection, with God, with the Church, and with those around you.

You were never meant to walk alone. You were made in the image of divine relationship.

Journal Prompt:

Are there relationships in your life that the Spirit is prompting you to restore or deepen? Are you staying connected to God and others?

"So God created humankind in his image, in the image of God he created them."
Genesis 1:27

Prayer:

Holy Trinity, You are a communion of love.

Thank You for making me in Your image, for relationship, not isolation.

Heal where I've pulled away.

Restore where there's been distance.

Help me to live connected to You, to others, and to who You've made me to be.

Let my life reflect the harmony and love of Your divine life.

Father, I ask this in Jesus' name, through the power of your Holy Spirit.

Amen.

DAY 9 – THE SPIRIT PRAYS WITHIN US

Devotional Reflection:

Sometimes, when life is overwhelming or painful, words fail us. We want to pray, but we don't know what to say. That's where the Holy Spirit meets us, not with judgment, but with comfort. The Spirit prays within us.

Romans 8:26 says, "The Spirit helps us in our weakness… that very Spirit intercedes with sighs too deep for words." What a gift that is. The Holy Spirit doesn't just prompt us to pray, He joins us in it. He speaks when we can't. He carries our groans, our confusion, our longing, directly to the heart of the Father.

Prayer isn't always eloquent. It's often messy. But because the Spirit dwells in us, even our silence can become a sacred offering. Even our sighs are heard in heaven. The Catechism describes the Spirit as "the interior Master of Christian prayer" (CCC 2672), reminding us that we don't pray to the Spirit, but we pray in the Spirit.

In my own life, I've had moments in prayer where all I could do was sit quietly and say, "Holy Spirit, help me." And He did. Not always with immediate answers, but always with peace. With clarity. With strength to take the next step.

You don't need perfect words today. You need openness. The Spirit will meet you where you are, not where you think you should be.

So, whether you're overflowing with praise or feeling empty and dry, the Spirit is ready to pray within you.

Journal Prompt:

Have you ever experienced prayer without words, just a quiet awareness of God? Reflect on what the Spirit may be praying in you today.

"The Spirit helps us in our weakness… with sighs too deep for words."
Romans 8:26

Prayer:

Holy Spirit, I don't always know how to pray.

But You do.

Intercede within me.

Carry the things I can't express to the Father.

When I am silent, pray through me.

When I am lost, lead me.

Make my heart a place where heaven hears even the smallest cry.

Thank You for praying with me and for me.

Father, I ask this in Jesus' name, through the power of your Holy Spirit.

Amen.

DAY 10 – THE SPIRIT MAKES US ONE

Devotional Reflection:

The Holy Spirit doesn't just work within individuals. He builds unity in the Body of Christ. He is the Spirit of communion, sent by the Trinity to make us one, not in uniformity, but in love.

At Pentecost, when the Spirit descended, people from every nation heard the Gospel in their own language. It wasn't confusion, it was unity in diversity. That's the work of the Spirit: gathering the scattered, healing divisions, building the Church.

Paul writes in 1 Corinthians 12:13, "In the one Spirit we were all baptized into one body." That includes every background, every story, every type of person. The Spirit makes us brothers and sisters, not strangers or competitors.

The Catechism tells us, "The Holy Spirit is the principle of every vital and truly saving action in each part of the Body" (CCC 798). That means He is not just working in me or in you, He is working in us. Together. Forming us into something greater than we could ever be alone.

This has challenged me. Sometimes I've preferred to go it alone, to stay in my comfort zone. But the Spirit always pulls me back into community. Into the Church.

Into relationship. Because the Christian life was never meant to be a solo journey.

The Spirit will stretch us, asking us to forgive, to collaborate, to walk with others we might not have chosen. But in doing so, He shapes us into the image of Christ.

Let Him draw you into unity today. If there's tension, seek peace. If there's isolation, seek connection. The Spirit is making us one.

Journal Prompt:

How is the Spirit inviting you to strengthen your connection to the Body of Christ? Is there someone you need to reconcile with?

"For in the one Spirit we were all baptized into one body."
1 Corinthians 12:13

Prayer:

Holy Spirit, build unity in me and through me.

Where there is division, sow peace.

Where there is distance, draw together.

Help me see others as You see them, part of the same body, beloved in Your eyes.

Use me to build up, not tear down.

Make us one, just as the Trinity is one.

Father, I ask this in Jesus' name, through the power of your Holy Spirit.

Amen.

DAY 11 – THE SPIRIT TEACHES TRUTH

Devotional Reflection:

In a world full of opinions, noise, and half-truths, the Holy Spirit leads us to what is real. He doesn't just inform us. He transforms us with truth. Jesus called Him "the Spirit of truth" (John 16:13) and promised that He would guide us into all truth, not just once, but continually.

The Catechism says, "The Holy Spirit… leads into all truth and, in communion with him, the whole truth of God is found" (CCC 243). This is not abstract theology, it's a personal invitation to live in God's reality. Truth isn't a concept. It's a Person. Jesus said, "I am the truth" (John 14:6), and the Spirit helps us know Him more fully.

When we invite the Spirit to lead our thoughts, He brings clarity where there is confusion. He convicts our hearts, not to condemn, but to bring freedom. I've had moments in prayer where Scripture illuminated something in my life I needed to change. That wasn't guilt. That was truth, and it set me free.

Sometimes the truth the Spirit reveals is comforting. Sometimes it's confronting. But it's always loving. And it always draws us closer to the Father and the Son.

Ask the Spirit today to teach you. Not just academically, but personally. He knows what you need to understand. He knows what truth will set you free.

Journal Prompt:

Is there an area in your life where you're seeking clarity, discernment, or truth? Ask the Spirit to guide you.

"When the Spirit of truth comes, he will guide you into all the truth."
John 16:13

Prayer:

Spirit of truth, teach me today.

Guide my thoughts, illuminate Your Word, and lead me in the way of Jesus.

Where I've believed lies, speak freedom.

Where I've doubted, bring confidence.

Help me to walk in truth, not just know it, but live it.

Lead me deeper into Your light and let that light shine in me.

Father, I ask this in Jesus' name, through the power of your Holy Spirit.

Amen.

DAY 12 – LIVING IN THE TRINITY'S LOVE

Devotional Reflection:

To live in the Spirit is to live in the love of the Trinity. Not just to believe in God, but to dwell in Him. To live from His love, every moment of every day.

1 John 4:16 tells us, "God is love, and those who abide in love abide in God, and God abides in them." The Catechism explains that "the ultimate end of the whole divine economy is the entry of God's creatures into the perfect unity of the Blessed Trinity" (CCC 260). This is the goal, not just salvation, but union. Not just faith, but communion.

The Spirit draws us into that divine embrace. He teaches us to live in love, not just emotionally, but intentionally. When we walk in the Spirit, we're not chasing religious experiences, we're living in relationship with a God who is Father, Son, and Holy Spirit.

There have been days when I've felt distant from God, unsure of what He wanted from me. But the more I lean into prayer, the more I realize: God wants me. Not my performance. Not my perfection. Just me. And through the Spirit, I find that I'm already being held in love.

That's what the Trinity offers, a life immersed in divine love. A life of belonging, of surrender, of joy. You don't have to earn it. You just have to receive it.

So today, live aware that you are surrounded, filled, and held by love.

Journal Prompt:

What does it look like for you to live from love today, not striving, but abiding?

"God is love, and those who abide in love abide in God, and God abides in them."
1 John 4:16

Prayer:

Holy Trinity, I want to live in Your love.

Help me to rest in the truth that I belong to You.

Let Your love shape my thoughts, my words, and my actions.

Draw me deeper into Your heart Father, Son, and Spirit.

Let my life be a reflection of the communion I've been invited into.

Father, I ask this in Jesus' name, through the power of your Holy Spirit.

Amen.

.

DAY 13 –TIME OF PRAYER: THE SPIRIT LIVES IN ME

Devotional Reflection:

As we close this theme on the Trinity and the Holy Spirit, we pause to remember one simple truth: the Spirit of God lives in you.

Not visits. Not observes. Lives.

This truth should shape how we pray, how we decide, how we walk into the day. We are temples of the Holy Spirit. Wherever we go, we carry the presence of God.

This does not mean life will always feel easy. It means we are never alone. The Spirit is the Comforter, the Guide, the Advocate. He reminds us who we are, children of the Father, followers of the Son, bearers of divine presence.

Today, sit in that reality. Say, "Holy Spirit, live in me fully." Invite Him into the everyday spaces. Into the ordinary. Let this be a day of awareness, a day to walk with the Spirit moment by moment.

The Trinity is not just a doctrine. It is your daily dwelling.

Prayer Focus:

Pray this slowly and sincerely:

Holy Spirit, I welcome You into every part of me. Be at home in my thoughts, my desires, and my steps today.

"Do you not know that your body is a temple of the Holy Spirit within you?"
1 Corinthians 6:19

Closing Prayer:

Holy Spirit, You live in me.

Let me never forget Your nearness.

Fill every room of my heart with Your peace.

Let me walk today with awareness, with joy, and with quiet confidence.

Make my life a reflection of the God who dwells within.

Father, I ask this in Jesus' name, through the power of your Holy Spirit.

Amen.

DAY 14: GO DEEPER ON SUNDAYS

You can watch this week's message at [BruceDownes.org]

A WORD BEFORE YOU GO

You've come to the end of the first part of this journey and what a sacred journey it has been.

Over these six weeks, we've reflected on the transforming presence of the Holy Spirit. We've seen how the Spirit doesn't only empower the Church at Pentecost, He empowers you, right here, right now. His strength is made perfect in your weakness. His presence is available every single day.

We've looked at how the Holy Spirit doesn't just fill us with power. He forms us with fruit. Love, joy, peace, patience, kindness, generosity, faithfulness, gentleness, and self-control. These are not goals to achieve, but gifts that grow when we stay connected to Him. Even when the growth feels slow, the Spirit is faithfully at work beneath the surface.

And we've opened our hearts to the mystery of the Trinity, Father, Son, and Holy Spirit, not as an idea, but as a living relationship. You were created by the Father, redeemed by the Son, and are now filled with the Spirit. This is the life we are meant for: a life immersed in divine love.

You may have started this journey feeling uncertain or even dry. But along the way, something deeper has been stirring. That's the Holy Spirit. And He is not finished with you.

If you continue into the next Series, you'll go further into the life of prayer and the leading of the Spirit. But even if you pause here, know this:

The Spirit who came at Pentecost comes for you.

The fruit He grows in others, He is growing in you.

And the love shared in the Trinity has been poured into your heart.

So, keep praying, **Come, Holy Spirit.**

Keep listening. Keep following.

And above all, stay open.

God is not done. He is only just beginning.